Is It Me
Or
Is It You

Is It Me Or Is It You

Observations, Opinions & Advice On Life,
Love and Relationships

WENDELL WALKER

authorHOUSE®

AuthorHouse™
1663 Liberty Drive
Bloomington, IN 47403
www.authorhouse.com
Phone: 1-800-839-8640

Published by AuthorHouse   11/08/2012

ISBN: 978-1-4772-8155-0 (sc)
ISBN: 978-1-4772-8154-3 (hc)
ISBN: 978-1-4772-8156-7 (e)

Library of Congress Control Number: 2012919491

DEDICATION

This book is dedicated to my daughters:

Antionette

Dale

Marquita

and

Laverne

ACKNOWLEDGEMENTS

First, I want to thank my friend and editor-for-life, Dr. E. Lee Lassiter, who helped put this book together. He has been a true friend from the time we met. My sincere gratitude goes out to him.

I also want to express my deep appreciation to another longtime friend, Mrs. Gail Lucas Tilman, who typed some of the chapters.

Special thanks to Geanna Franqui for helping me with my emails.

Finally, I want to acknowledge the assistance of Mrs. Elenora Morton who typed several chapters.

CONTENTS

FOREWORD

Some things work. Some things don't. Some things help you. Other things hurt you. But, in all things, be positive. Together, the three thoughts sum up the author's view of what it takes to make it—in life in general and, especially, in personal relationships.

How did he come by this wisdom? First, he credits a stern foster mother. From her he learned about rules and consequences. Second, as he grew up with 16 siblings in her ". . . house of many beatings . . . ," he became a keen observer of how differently people deal with their circumstances.

Observing and learning became a way of life as he played soldier in the U.S. and Vietnam, survived a marriage that ended early and tragically, and pursued a bumpy-road dream of becoming a successful businessman—beginning with $2.

Through it all, he learned to value self-appreciation and self-reliance, honesty and hard work, respect for other people and the importance of love and laughter, patience, understanding, and a willingness to help others.

Is It Me Or Is It You deals with the ticklish topic of relationships. It catalogues a wide-range of the author's observations, opinions, and advice on the subject. Occasionally, the views venture into the realms of life and love in general.

While he does not portray himself as an expert, he paints a clear picture of what he has seen or lived—the good, the bad, and the ugly—and speaks as an authority on what he believes it all means.

Sometimes—to borrow one of the author's favorite words—the advice is harsh and hard hitting. But, most often, the bed of wit and humor on which it is served makes it digestible. For example, he says, some men are so selfish, maybe they should have married themselves.

That is not Dr. Phil. It is Wendell Walker as you will get know him in Is It Me Or Is It You: One man—driven by a deep concern for the sad state of relationships in the world today—daring to become a voice crying in the wilderness, whatever the consequences.

Bear in mind that Is It Me Or Is It You is a two-way conversation. You get to have your say after you have finished the book.

—The Author

INTRODUCTION

I am not writing this book for myself. It is intended to help those people who are forever complaining about the flaws, faults, and failings of their "relationships".

I sincerely hope my views prove to be a benefit to people in that group who see their own faults and want to make amends, to make things right.

I want you to see the real "you" in what you are doing and the part you may be playing—without realizing it—in how your relationships turn out.

Many relationships fail because a "third party" is let into the picture: not a person but such outside influences as opinions and hearsay. I am saying: Think about your life as if no one existed but the two of you.

How would you treat your mate, your friend, your companion—then? How would you like to be treated?

Finally, maybe what I have to say will help you relate to your children and to how life really exists. Perhaps, I can to steer you away from the mistakes that so many adults allow to destroy what could have been a beautiful relationship.

Wendell Walker

Chapter One

Get Ready Get Set Go

—1—
CHAPTER

I Want to Be Close to You

Love

What is love? Is it a mutual feeling between a man and a woman? A feeling that makes their hormones jump when they meet?

Where do such feelings come from? Is it a mental thing? What makes people go all out to please each other, to make sure what they feel is showing through.

Is that the thing they call love? Where exactly does the magic begin? What sparks the kind of fire that makes two people want to give a relationship their all?

Love has so many sides, it should come with directions: It causes jealousy, distrust, worry, stress, loss of appetite, headaches, and long sleepless nights.

People miss work, resort to stalking, leave home, go to jail and get sick "unto death" all in the name of love. It is enough to make you wonder why people try it again and again.

That question leads to another. If love is so strong between two people, what makes it go away so suddenly when one gets mad at the other?

What makes it go away in a spur of the moment? Love is not meant to be flipped on and off like a light switch. Was it love in the beginning or just a slow road to sex.

Some of us want more and keep the spark alive so that the feeling can grow. Others seem to move on to the next victim—getting hurt or hurting others as they go.

Sometimes, it seems that everything everyone does is wrong: something one or the other says has an unexpected and unintended effect and it hurts down to the soul.

Love makes some people argue a lot. It keeps going and going as each one tries to out do the other in the hurt feelings department. Stuff from months, even years past is brought up all over again.

Arguments often lead to abuse in one form or the other. The results can go far beyond bruised feelings. Simply put, love is not good all the time.

The pain—real or rational or not—makes some people run. "I love you, but I cannot see you no more." Such statements are painful to hear.

Do you realize what you have done to that person? Sometimes, they ask in all honesty: What did I do for you to leave?

The answer, most of the time, is "nothing. It is me." Well, what more does it take when you have been given all the love there was to give?

Stop thinking that a relationship is like turning off a light: Off and it is as if it never existed; On again and everything becomes new and starts all over.

Sex

Sex is really for reproduction and to help replenish the earth. Take a walk with me, look at the insects. All they do is have sex and eat. Look at the animals. They have sex and eat. Do they just have sex for fun?

We humans have taken sex out of context. We are not looking to reproduce; we are looking for a good time. This is not all bad, if . . . . Big IF. If it is pleasing on both sides, not as some men see it: I got mine, where were you?

That attitude is off the mark. Now he has taken it out of proportion. He is just looking for his little three minutes and he is okay. Then he wonders why she is upset, not just for a minute but stays mad for one or two weeks.

He is walking around with his head up as if he has done his job. He does not realize that he has only left her frustrated. She did not even get a kiss out of this.

Women want to be put in the mood, which is called foreplay. Make her feel wanted; make her passion explode. Make her feel like she is going to the extreme.

When she reaches her peak and you reach yours, the result is two happy people. Sex is not a one-sided thing. It takes two people.

What makes a lot of women deny they want or need sex? They parade excuses: I have a headache or the little kitten is in town. Why not just say I am not in the mood. Eventually, he goes elsewhere and she is mad. She ran him out.

Be open and upfront. Explain to each other what you like and what you do not like, do and don't do. Then, there are no surprises.

Do not get upset if one or the other says I do not do that. Find ways to please each other that are mutually acceptable. Usually there is enough common ground for a lifetime of sexual happiness.

Today, some women say they do not need a man. I have my toys. That leaves some men sputtering with resentment but then there is this to consider: men are in short supply.

Why is that? One third is locked up and the military machine is killing another third. Only one third is left. Women outnumber men 15 to one.

Perhaps, toys make sense under the circumstances. Some women turn to lesbianism at a young age. Today, when a man enters a relationship, he does know what he has gotten himself into.

Sex plays a key role in a relationship. The lack of it can make either or both parties seek it some where else. Men are being lovers of men, and women are doing the same. What is next?

When a man or woman finds someone who is straight, the right thing to do is work hard to keep the relationship going. It is a miracle when anyone finds a person who really cares. Usually, it is the little things that count most.

A man feels that when a woman refuses to have sex, she has somebody else. He feels certain about it when once a week turns into once a month, then nothing. He may have it all wrong.

He walks with his head down. All kinds of visions spin around in it. Knowing that he has done nothing wrong, he keeps asking himself: why is she rejecting me?

What should you do in this situation? Just be truthful. Tell him what the problem really is. It might be a health-related condition that you are reluctant to bring up. If you wait too long it might be too late.

When the woman is the one rejected, she reacts the same as a man. The first thing that comes to her mind is, he has somebody else. That is not always the case. He too could be tired or have a health problem.

Lack of communication can cause a break up. In the end, both parties are sorry when they realize the worrying was for the wrong reason. Each thinks, when will I have sex again? Do they still want me? How can I tell them I am sorry?

In both of their hearts, all they really wanted was to please each other.

What Do You Want . . . .

Question
What are you looking for in a relationship?

---

1. What do I see in this person?

2. What do I like about this person?

3. What draws me to this person?

4. Do they have a job?

5. Is their clothing always in place?

6. Are they a shop-a-holic?

7. Are they responsible?

8. Are they good providers?

9. Do they pay their bills on time?

10. Will they like my children?

11. How much money do they have?

12. Will they really care for me?

13. Do they have a lot of baggage?

14. Do you think they might be an abuser?

15. Is it all about me, me, me . . . one sided?

16. Will they change after we meet?

17. Are they controlling?

18. Are they the jealous type?

19. Will I have my freedom?

20. Will my life stop if we get together?

21. Will I be their slave?

22. Do they love their car more than me?

23. Do they like to be cuddled?

24. Will they make time for me?

25. Are they a "Mommy's Child"?

26. Will I ever go anywhere outside of the USA?

27. What is in their plan for me?

28. Are they a gambler, drinker, smoker?

29. Are they doing drugs?

30. Will they steal from me?

31. Are they clean?

32. Are they all about their friends; will I be neglected?

33. Do they like to argue all the time?

34. Do they have a goal in life?

35. Do they have a purpose just to be living?

36. Do they want children?

37. Do they value a dollar?

38. Do they value their job?

39. Are they good planners?

40. Will they love me for me?

41. Will they respect me?

42. Do they have common sense?

Religion and Your Relationship

Religion plays a very important part in a relationship. There are the true believers, and those who just believe when you are around. What you believe in is between you and God.

Your relationship with God is significant. Do not let it ruin your relationship; do not, for example, let it lead you to neglect your mate. If you cannot cope with your mate because religion has gone to your head, why not become a priest or nun?

Some people neglect their mate and claim that God told them this or that. It seems strange that they are that close to God but can not get along with their mate. They are always stressed out over little things and push the mate to the side.

Many people take religion to the extreme. They seem to think that God only talks to them then leaves everyone else on the sideline. Yet, when a problem comes up, their faith is nowhere to be found.

They sit there as if God is going to knock on the door and say, "I got your rent money." They make no effort to help themselves. Their hope goes down the drain and they forget all about religion.

God put us down here with a little bit of Himself in all of us. But, sometimes, our minds lead us to see and hear what is not there. We say a voice in me told me this or that. God made us human, not saints.

Your mate is a human being. God gave you a mind to think, to praise Him for His goodness—and to honor your mate. That holds true, even if you are a preacher, Bishop, or whatever name you choose.

Arguments keep going and get out of hand because neither mate wants to give in first. If people say what they have to say and leave it alone, things work out much better.

Some believers say, "I took my problems to God and left them there." Why not leave your problems where they started. Other believers "believe" only when they are around you. They agree with everything you say.

They know enough Bible verses to make you think that they are true believers. They want you to believe they went to school with Jesus before the disciples. The big thing for them is to avoid open drama with their mate.

They only put up a front when they are around you. They live in this world with you. They still believe in somebody, but it is not as in the open as you "real believers."

A lot of people use religion just to get over, to get by. They are weak-minded when it comes to the subject. Many bad deals are made by using religion and Christianity as a cover.

When we read the Bible, we think that everybody in it was a saint. Wrong. There were liars, thieves, murderers, cut-throats, whores, and non-believers. Fortunately, some of them made a change.

It is not wise to think now is better than then, that people are different today. In a relationship, look at your own faults. Be as one with your mate and let

God lead you. Do not try to lead God because you think he is too slow about getting to you.

We should stop trying to rush life in general, not just in our love life. Sometimes, you have to "mark time", that is, just march in place the way soldiers do until your time comes. You are not forgotten, it is just not your time.

What is for you in life, you are going to get. No one can stop it. Your life was cut and dried before you came into existence. The right and wrong choices that we make shape the journey but do determine our destiny.

We hear the claim sometimes that a person's life was cut short. But, was it really? Your time is your time, enjoy the moment, enjoy the beauty, and enjoy what life has given you—especially, if you have your mind and your health.

What we read in the Bible—those things we think those people did wrong—is there to improve your chance at getting it right in your life. Just remember that you and your mate are one.

15

In a relationship, if one person believes in religion and the other does not, this can cause a big conflict. The non-believer may make remarks like these:

"You know that stuff is not real. Have you seen God? What has He done for you? Why then are we living like this? Why are we always arguing and fighting?" You believe in all that and you are not any better than I am.

The response will sound something like this: "Look. Who woke you up this morning? How is it you are talking? Why are you walking?" Why this and why that. But the unbeliever remains just as unconvinced as ever.

Do not push anyone to believe in religion. Let them make that choice. If one of you is Baptist and the other is Catholic, do not try to force one or the other to change. You cannot change anybody. It boils down to this: You are blessed if both believe in something.

Closer to Home

Myself

I was born June 13, 1944 in Roanoke, Virginia. I was born at 226 Walker Avenue North East. At the age of six, I went to a foster home where I remained until I finished high school.

During my childhood, my foster mother engraved in my mind how a woman is supposed to be treated. She did not know a whole lot, but what she did know she gave to me.

This is a quote she repeated often: "If you take a girl out and she does not get home, don't you come back. You pick her up at her door and you bring her back to her door."

At that age, I didn't even have a girlfriend, not in high school. However, I had a mind that wondered what life would bring me. I always looked forward to having someone to be my queen, someone to provide for.

I was so poor at the time, I just existed. There was no other side to the world. We went to school and back home. Working in the field was like being in jail. I heard people saying, "Jesus is the way." The strap was the way in our house. It seems that everything we did was wrong.

I went into the Army in 1962 and was discharged in 1965. I lived in Washington State for a year and worked on the railroad. I came to Baltimore that year with $2.00 to my name.

After I had been in Baltimore a couple of months or so, my sister took me to a night club. Going to the club became a pleasant outing for me. I would watch the musician play. I learned to play the organ. I played with many bands and later formed my own band.

I went into business in 1968 as a Home Improvement Contractor. I only had $5.00 in capital. Faith is so powerful, I did not realize I was not suppose to make it. I am still in business today.

To be significant in life means a lot to me. I cherish being able to put my all in all in whatever I do. Praising God at all times gives me the energy to keep going. I am grateful to God for what I turned out to be.

I know how to treat a woman. I am from the old school. A man should provide for his family, which I do with honors. The woman should not have to tell her man everything to do. Common sense should do that.

Communication plays a great part in a successful relationship but love is the main ingredient. Ninety-five percent of the time, I am happy and contented. The other five percent I spend wondering why.

My Relationships

I met my mate in 1979 while plying my trade as a Home Improvement Contractor. I was called to paint the exterior of her house.

I did not speak much while I was working. I just went about my business trying to make my work presentable. I had no idea a relationship would come out of it.

After I finished the job and she was pleased, we exchanged phone numbers. We started going out to a few places. I still did not look for anything to come out of it, but I did feel that she was one beautiful woman.

She was soft spoken. A glow in her eyes drew me closer and closer. She was kind and never spoke a harsh word. I could feel the loving spirit that dwelled within her soul.

When I met my future mate, I had a three-year-old daughter. Her mother, my first wife, had died shortly after my daughter's birth. My daughter rejected my new friend in the beginning but after a few months they bonded.

In August 1980, we were married and we are still married today. We have never had an argument. We always give each other compliments. She is very respectful and caring towards me and shows her gratitude for everything I do for her.

Being from the old school, I believe a man should provide for his family. That is me. I am a great provider. I take care of our home and family. I take care of all the bills. I do not want her to worry about a thing. I do not want her to want for anything.

She is always treated as my queen. I do not go overboard with the finances that we have. I give her my love, respect, and my care. We never interfere in each other's business. We feel secure in each other.

Her biggest worry is her family; my worry is about her not having to worry about me. My goal in life is to keep her happy and secure.

We all have negative thoughts at times. They are kept at the thought stage. We do not have to let them surface. We are so busy pleasing each other and keeping each other smiling and laughing, our life is enjoyable.

People should not let their life be a stumbling block for their mate. If you see it becoming one, move it and nobody will fall. I am not saying that we are living a perfect life, but we are striving for perfection.

As for me, I do not need a whole lot. Give me God's love, her love, my family's love, and the love of 90% of my friend's. What more can you ask for. I have never been selfish toward her or anybody else.

When you let yourself go completely with your mate and they do the same, you become connected. It is as if you are reading each other's mind. Yet, we give each other all the space in the world.

We go and come as we please. What time did you get in or where have you been is never asked. Freedom is just what it means. Most people have been held back so long they do not know what freedom really means. We do not have to look over our shoulder watching each other.

Treat your mate the way you want to be treated. I say that knowing that some people do not seem to give a damn how they are treated. Sometimes you have to adopt the good qualities that you see in somebody else. Do not be afraid to ask questions. Pride will keep you at the bottom of the pit.

We are asked often, "How do you all stay so loving, always with smiles on your faces? Is it that you are just meant for each other?" What do you do? You may get the same or similar questions. Do not be selfish. Give a helping hand or advice. At least you tried.

Just remember your relationship is yours; it may not work for nobody else. What keeps you smiling may not seem funny to anyone else. Do what you do from your heart always for your mate. Sometimes, we go a lifetime trying to please each other, and not please ourselves.

We do things, knowing that we cannot afford it. We are going out of our way to do it just for one to be pleased, but they are not. See, your mind is telling you, if I do not do this or that, he or she might leave me.

In addition, not all you have done came from your heart. You are trying to buy love, it did not work. Just be a man or woman, and say I cannot afford it right now. I pray for that day when I can. One of you becomes selfish, and your relationship becomes one-sided.

When you first met, neither of you had anything, but the love for each other was strong. You did not care what each other had at that moment. When the relationship began, all you worried about was seeing each other.

Reality sets in and you have little or nothing. You want to give each other the world, knowing that you do not own it. Do not make promises you cannot keep.

Make your relationship grow; do a little at a time. It is like building a house. You start with the foundation and build upon it. When years have passed, you can look back and say: Remember when . . . ?"

Life is only as hard as you make it. Be there for each other. That makes life complete.

". . . your relationship is yours, it may not work for anyone else . . ."

Wendell Walker

Is It Me Or Is It You?

Chapter Two

Under the influence Of eden

—2—

CHAPTER

Under the Influence of Eden

Young Love

The younger generation has to learn what love really is. For them, it is all about sex, getting high, drinking and such that turns them on. There is no respect

25

for the woman. Her name has become bitch, whore, and whatever other names her man can think up. Of course, his name is "dog" or something similar.

Responsibility is not in their vocabulary. Their cars become their god. Money is like water to them; it just pours. The woman is treated as though slavery has come back, especially if the man is a control freak.

Work is a myth. Washing dishes does not exist. They are lazy and do not want to work or accept responsibility. They have no get up and go. Their whole world consists of sex, sleep, and play.

There are exceptions, of course. Some young people try to get it together. They look at their friends just going to the dogs and they try to change their life. Some work, have spunk, and want something out of life. But, generally, certain relationship ideas are way off base.

The first point I want to make is this: When you met this man or woman, they had a name. Continue to call them by that name. And, regarding slavery, remember that back when, we did not have a choice. Now we do.

Your man or woman is not in slavery now. Do not lower yourself to be treated as one. There is more to life than sex, getting high, loud music, rapping, and automobiles with tinted-windows.

To Be, Not To Be and Wanna Be

The fairy-book relationship most of us say we want does not just pop up like Spring flowers in Eve's Garden of Eden. But, you can "grow" a great relationship. You are the key. How you "play" you is what matters.

Be yourself at all times. Sometimes, people may think you are silly. Some may say you are crazy. But, on-stage and off, be you. What the song says about "different strokes for different folks" is right on the money.

Most often, you are accepted when you are being yourself. There may be a time when you are rejected. Do not let it worry you. Weigh your positive qualities against the negative ones and you will find reasons to move on.

A positive "To Be . . ." attitude about life makes a lot of things fall into place for you. It seems that everything you touch turns to gold. This is very much the case in relationships.

When a man and a woman walk onto the stage of life with a "To Be" attitude and both want something out of life, they become winners. They take what life hands them and build the life they desire to have.

On the other hand, a "Not To Be" way of thinking has just the opposite effect.

Dwelling on the negative side of life makes you feel that nothing in your life is in line. You declare: "I cannot do this or that because . . ." or ". . . they are not going to give me a loan or whatever . . ."

Your negative attitude keeps you from getting what life has promised you. You go through life missing out on everything life has for you. However, the rejection is your own doing.

Your life is an open book of "ifs" and "should ofs." You will have been born, lived, and died without leaving even a footprint in the sands of time.

"Wanna Be" people live a two-sided life. They lie constantly about having been around the world and seen and done everything, at least once. They own everything that can possibly be owned. Whatever the subject, they have ". . . been there, done that."

When the "Wanna Be" person meets someone of the opposite sex, lies pour out like water. They have no problem lying and making promises. They promise the sky and throw in the world just to sweeten the pot.

They have a plane in the hanger, just in case they choose to go somewhere in a hurry. They own a yacht on the bay, should they want to take a slow boat to China.

They own a car lot and can select any car on it if they need to run to the market. They own the city, so they can pick and choose any sidewalk for an exclusive stroll.

They live in a world of fantasy.

At times, they want to be you. They envy you so much you become their fantasy. Tomorrow, it is somebody else. It is not surprising that their idea of a relationship is less than realistic.

Now comes the moment of truth: man meets woman, woman meets man. A relationship begins to form. It is time to take a ride in that airplane that never existed. However, the only thing flying is a squadron of excuses: The plane is being worked on; the price of gas went up.

Well, what about that boat ride? Trot out some excuse that won't hold water. Let's go for a ride in the country. The car lot went bankrupt. Can we just take a walk? The city has banned walking.

The next man or woman may well catch hell because of the hurt feelings this kind of behavior leaves behind. But, you cannot stop there. Life involves risks. Don't hate yourself for the rest of your life if you are the one who fell for the lies.

Give yourself a reality check. Maybe you were just out-played. Maybe there was not enough time for you to run your game all the way out. Too many people play games that undermine relationships before they get off the ground. Being real is the better way.

Pleased to Make Your Acquaintance

What did you see in this man when you first laid eyes on him—probably when he was not looking? What was the attraction that made you want him to be yours, even before you had your first conversation with him?

You saw him, your eyes and face lit up, your hormones ran wild, and all kinds of thoughts ran through your mind. Then, somehow or another, the day comes when you meet him and have a conversation.

Was the conversation interesting? Was it enjoyable simply because he seemed to be saying just what you wanted to hear? Whatever the case, before the close of the day, he asks you: "May I see you again?"

Of course, you say, "Yes". After all, this is what you wanted.

You meet for the second time. Now, the conversation changes. It is all about him. You hardly got a word in. You think: What in the hell have I gotten myself into? You saw everything you wanted, until the mouth opened. Then, you were turned off.

Will you give him another chance or do you end it right there? Next time, maybe you will get the opportunity to express yourself. Not giving him another chance could lead to "I should have stayed in it longer" regrets.

Did you miss something in the first conversation? What is it that makes you want to see this man again anyway?

You may have to go through 10 or 15 "getting acquainted" routines in order to find the man or woman for you.

Too many people play games that undermine relationships before they get off the ground.

Wendell Walker

Is It Me Or Is It You?

Chapter Three

Who You Looking At . . .

—3—
CHAPTER

Who You Looking At . . .

Are You This Woman Or Man?

The two of them seem to enjoy life to the fullest. They embrace life and each other and appreciate every moment life gives them. They thank each other graciously for everything that is done—gifts, favors, gestures.

They both work hard and leave drama out of the relationship. They are so calm and laidback, they do not have time to feel insecure. Jealousy does not enter into their minds.

We all make choices in our lives. Some of us stray from our plans in life; some remain steadfast and determined to get something out of it. Building a relationship becomes easier if the man and woman care for life and people.

When a man or woman comes with a "I do not give a damn" attitude, what can you expect to come out of it. If you put nothing into a relationship, how are you going to get anything out of it?

When you see a man and woman enjoying people, laughing, and joking and displaying a glow in their eyes for each other, it is because they realize that life is short. They are trying to live it to the fullest.

Both persons have to give and take in a relationship. Things cannot be one-sided with one person always on the receiving end. Think beyond the moment and show appreciation at all times. "Thank You" costs nothing. Gratitude goes a long way.

Think back on your life. When you were given a piece of candy, you gave thanks from your heart. Do things from the heart. Not everything has a price. Ask yourself the question often: What can I do to show my thanks?

This formula is not magic. You can do everything you are asked to do and can think to do and still one day hear: I do not need you any more. In spite of this possibility, continue to spread it on. Do things from the heart until the cup "runneth" over.

The Unpredictable Woman

A man meets a woman and everything seems to click between them. They are going out and eating out without tension or disagreement. There is joy and laughter, everything is overwhelmingly pleasant.

Out of the blue, she changes for no reason except she seems to want to be in control.

Conversing becomes tricky because it is now hard to know what words, topics, and issues are off-limits. Then, in a few minutes, she is back to "normal" and acting as if everything is fine.

The man is baffled by the quick changes.

He thinks he has done something wrong. She assures him he has not. Fearing he will say the wrong thing, he is lost for words. He wonders: Does she have issues? Should I leave before things get worse. What have I gotten myself into?

Men need to have an open mind in situations of this sort and learn to expect the unexpected. They must be alert, secure, and prepared to accept what ever comes next. Sometimes, to his surprise, something in his soul may make him want to reach out for more.

The man may begin to fall in love with this woman, over looking her "faults." Everyday, she is all he can think about, knowing now that everyday may just bring a surprise. He has learned to take the good with the bad. She is caring, has a good heart and much more.

Changing—day-to-day, moment-to-moment—is the way of the woman. What you see is not always what is there. It is like boys and girls in grade school—watch out for the ones that "fight" each other all the time. Usually, it is just a matter of time.

Women change faces as a shield, as a way to protect themselves. It is a means of keeping their guard up. When they know in their heart they are falling, they decide, I cannot tell him just yet. I can only show him a little at a time. That is why they make everyday a surprise.

They want to be kissed and held—for a few minutes—then realize: Oh, I have let my guard down again. They change. Their feelings for the person are still growing stronger. What makes these things happen?

Men are just the puppets; women work the strings. They have complete control. Men can do nothing without them. She has the first word and the last. We cannot kiss her unless she says okay; we cannot call, go out, hang around, or have sex without her say so.

They tell us when to come and when to go. That is why they are unpredictable. They are the boss. Men are the workers. Eve did it to Adam. Men have been followers ever since.

The Half and Half Woman

Her first half: She steps out of her house looking like the Queen of England. Her clothing fits her to a tee, her hair looks like a picture you just cut out of a magazine.

Her face glows: It is like an open door with a soft light coming in. Her walk turns men's heads all the way around. She loves attention and stays in men's faces a lot.

She has the gift of gab and knows what to say and when to say it. She belongs to that band of women who likes to flirt—primarily to get attention.

She is respectable and trustworthy and has good manners.

Now comes the other half: You cannot get into her house. She is nasty and does not clean up. Dirty dishes are everywhere—on the sink, table and floor. She has not washed her clothes in months.

Her man is just the opposite. He is clean, tidy, and respectful to her and everybody else. For a time, he picks up behind her daily. But, eventually, he gets tired of tidying up after her and having to tell her to do this and that.

Finally, he starts throwing his stuff in the floor. He stops picking up behind her. Now she has brought him down to her level. She has control of his mind. He does not want to leave, stays on and deals with it. Why are some men so weak?

Of course, the scenario works in reverse sometimes. In either case, stop being half and half. Be complete.

The Genuine Woman

Here she comes radiating confidence and beauty.

She speaks softly at all times. The sound of her voice sparks vibrations in anyone listening.

She always walks with her head up.

She appreciates life and nature.

She reaches out readily—to give a helping hand to her man and sound advice to her children.

You feel her love as she talks. The words, the thoughts draw you into her web.

She goes about her day-to-day duties in an orderly and efficient manner. She keeps everything in place.

Her clothes fit her as if they were made just for her.

She goes about her job with a smile on her face at all times.

Her trust in God keeps her going. Her faith is overwhelming. Her hope is always a day ahead of tomorrow.

She appreciates everything that is done for her. A "Thank You" always follows a meal out, a movie or whatever is done for her.

She takes pride in everything that she does.

She looks at her man in a way that says: We are the only ones that exist. She always lifts him up, never resorts to using negative, downgrading words.

She is her own woman. She gives him space to be his own man.

The Genuine Man

This man is a proud man. He looks at life and nature and pulls beauty out of everything he sees. He is not boastful; he keeps a smile on his face as if it were painted on. He takes care of his woman and his household. Whatever is needed, he provides.

He walks erect. He looks at his woman with tenderness, with eyes they say: You are the only woman in this world that matters. Their communication is uplifting to both.

His trust in God gives him the courage to go on from day to day. His life has no dull moments. He likes to laugh and joke.

He lets the world know that he has pride. He lets it show in the way he goes on with his life. He does not carry around a lot of issues because he pushes all negativity to the back burner. He always has a positive attitude.

He encourages people to follow their dreams. He preaches: You will get what is for you in life. No one can stop you. You have choices in life. You are responsible for the roads you take. Do not blame others if you pick the wrong route to follow.

Procrastination will keep you at a stand still. One day you finally take a step but life will have passed you by. Have you ever thought about what our purpose in this world is?

God did not bring anyone here just to sit down while others wait on them. If you have no purpose in life, what is the point of being here?

The Insecure Woman

She loves her man so much that she hates to see him looking at someone else. She is always on edge. She cannot bear to see him with anyone but herself. She hates for him to go out alone because she finds herself walking the floor, wondering what he is doing.

He is always being accused of being involved with someone else. She picks an argument with her man on purpose although he takes care of the home, the bills and everything that goes with it.

Instead of showing gratitude to him, she does the opposite. One minute, she acts like a real woman but changes in the next. His talking on the phone triggers a barrage of questions or comments: Who is that? Why is she calling you? I know that is one of your whores.

The caller could have been his sister, a friend, or a business client. She secretly checks his phone to see who he calls. If the same number comes up frequently, her man's name is mud.

She becomes stressed out and cannot eat or sleep because of worrying about what he is doing. She hardly goes to work. If he works overtime, she calls to make sure he is there.

He tries hard to cope with this woman, to deal with her sickness, but nothing ever changes.

Lady, give him his space. Did you worry about him this way when you first met him? If you want him to put his trust in you, give him the same respect. While you are so busy thinking about what he is doing, maybe you need to look at yourself?

If he behaved exactly like you, how would you feel? Think about the energy you are wasting because of your insecurity and put it to some positive use. You do not realize that you are about to lose your man just by being stupid.

What made you start fantasizing in the first place? What happened to all the love that you had for him? If you had set out to have a positive outlook on life, you would not have time to spy on his life.

If he had a business that called for him to deal with women, you probably would commit suicide. If your drama causes him to walk out on you, you did it. Stop trying to control your mate. Start looking at your own faults and try to correct them.

The Insecure Man

This man is obsessed with himself; he believes that all life circles around him and his woman.

He tells her what and what not to wear. She cannot do anything by herself because jealousy has overcome him. He is always looking around the corner to see where she went.

She can hardly talk on the telephone more than five minutes before he starts getting frustrated. If she has company, he is uncomfortable. He clings to her like a blood-sucking leech day and night.

He tries to portray the image of being just the opposite of how he is but the jealousy is written all over his face. He shows up on her job unexpectedly and frequently accuses her of being with this or that man.

He is barely able to work on his own job because his mind is busy making up things to say to her when she gets home. He is constantly picking on or hollering at his woman.

She is in jail in her own house. If she speaks to the mailman in a soft voice, he suspects the worse and accuses her of it. Does a man this jealous belong in a relationship?

Sometimes, it is not all his fault, especially if he has a flirting woman. She is not actually doing anything but she just likes the attention. Of course, he cannot stand it.

He becomes a wild man and physical abuse is likely to follow. He threatens or tries to ". . . mess up her face . . ." to keep anyone else from wanting her.

One minute he is loving and caring. In a split second, he changes. After a violent outbreak, he is pleading for forgiveness and promising it will never happen again. But it does.

Why? What really causes this person to act this way? Answer: Insane jealousy, something few relationships can withstand.

The Selfish Woman

Here she comes. Looking like someone who just stepped out of Vogue Magazine. Everything is in place—her hair, clothes, shoes, purse and her gloves. Everything has to be just right.

Her man walks behind her like a puppy.

She is very controlling at all times. She almost tells him when to speak.

This man treats her like gold, but he gets none of the respect he deserves.

She does not ask him to do anything. She tells him.

When they go out for the evening, she treats him as if he is not there. She is in everybody's face throughout the night. When he sees her again, it is time to go home.

She has nothing to say to him in the car on the way home. Once they are in the house, she speaks but only to say: I am tired. Good night. In bed, they face in opposite directions.

He lies awake thinking: This woman has made me feel like something less than a man; she treats me like trash in spite of all that I do. I take care of home and the bills and do whatever needs to be done.

Sleepless for all or much of the night, he wonders: Have I met the Devil's advocate—maybe the Devil herself. What does she really need me for?

The Selfish Man

Here he comes, knowing more than Jesus. He has the answer to everything. His woman just exists around him. She picks up behind him, fixes his food, washes his cloths, and does everything else he tells her to do.

She is there for him, but he is not appreciative. The relationship is all about him. It is my this, my that, mine, mine, mine. Why didn't he marry himself?

This man has the answer to everything but does not have common sense. Because he gives her money—not a lot, mind you—he thinks she can do nothing without him.

He talks down to her and is very demanding. He cannot do anything for himself. He tries to make you think that he owns Home Depot and Lowes. He wants his friends to think that he is a millionaire and then some.

He tells his friends that he is the king of his ship. But, his house is really hers. In any discussion, he has the answer for everything. He knows everybody, from The President down.

He can barely make ends meet, but to hear him talk, he needs nothing, wants for nothing.

He pursues his dreams to the fullest while his woman waits, puts her dreams on hold in order to help him. When he gets where he is going, her dreams were for nothing because he does need her anymore. Goodbye.

The Confined Woman

She lives alone in her own domain; she finds it hard to cope with a man.

Sometimes she is very productive in what she does. She knows that her house will be kept in order. She does not have to worry about picking up behind a man.

She fears that if a man were around, he might be controlling and too much of an interference in her life. Her life-style might be brought to a stand still.

She says that she does not need a man; she can do badly by herself. The truth is that when those four walls start closing in on her at night, she wishes someone was there with her.

Sometimes it is this woman's fault that she does not have a man. Some women cannot live with anyone but themselves.

On the job, co-workers are led to believe that she has the best man in the world. He is her make-believe man. No one ever sees him. He is out-of-town on business or his absence is always somehow excused or accounted for.

(Then again, why do some women always let her man move in with them?)

Some claim they do not need a man because they have Jesus. They do not seem to realize that Jesus sent man down here for them? Jesus knew that when a woman needed someone to hold and kiss her, He would not be around.

Some women seem to think that religion is a substitute for the job a man is suppose to do. Actually, relationships work better when we let God do what He does and let man do what God put him here to do.

Some women live alone by choice for a variety of reasons. Some are afraid a man will infringe on their freedom. Will he create a jealousy jail? Will I have to tell him what to do all the time?

If he moves in, will he take over my home? Will he be responsible? Does he have two faces? Can he hold a job? What does he bring to the table? Is he a time-bomb that will go off and hurt me at the slightest touch.

Some confined women (most????) are afraid to get married. They have a lot of love to give and want someone with whom to share it, but a little voice in their heart keeps telling them to stay single.

Others stay in their world because that is where they need to be. They have issues—prior abuse, a disastrous childhood. For whatever reason, some women cannot stand anyone but themselves.

They get lonely and they have needs but it may be hard for them to let themselves go. Alone, they are at peace.

The Confined Man

He lives alone and, at times, wonders why.

Sometimes he chooses it; some live like a hermit.

Most of them do not want a steady woman. They like the variety of life.

Some just want the peace of mind that goes with being alone: No drama, no arguing, no outbursts, no being told what to do and when to do it, no pick this up, no do this or do that.

Some clean up behind themselves and some just exist. Some live on pizzas. Empty boxes litter their kitchen. They are just dirty and no self-respecting woman wants them. But, on the other hand, some women take what they can get.

Sometimes, this man is a Neatnik. He wants to keep everything in order. Some women can't take it. He is a clean freak. He may have had a bad experience with a woman that causes him to prefer his shell. He does not ever want to get married.

He likes to be able to come and go whenever and wherever he wants. He does not want to answer to anyone. He has needs but his mind and emotions make him wary of living with a woman. He thinks:

Is she going to trap me? Women are sneaky. Sometimes they get pregnant on purpose. She will do anything that comes to mind to get the man. She pulls out all the stops. She is a Scarlet O'Hara in her own time, a preying mantis that bites the head off the male after sex.

The confined man thinks of all of these things ahead of time. He stays focused on the unforeseen. He keeps himself alert at all times, keeps his guard up always. He knows the games that women play and keeps that to himself. He confines himself on purpose.

When a woman starts getting closer than he wants, he backs up again. The woman thinks that she has done something wrong. His behavior sometimes makes the woman decide something is wrong with him, that she cannot deal with it. She goes on about her business.

Some relationships are horrible and some are nice. It takes courage for a man to let himself go. When he does, she may hurt him on purpose if he does not become a "Yes Man." Sometimes, it is like being in the Army. As soon as he meets someone and starts getting close, he gets "shipped out."

This is uppermost in his mind when he enters the next relationship. He is always thinking: This is not going to last long. I am just here for the moment. It goes on and on until he becomes a bonafide, certified Confined Man.

The Possessive Woman

She is ordinary. There is nothing extraordinary about her at the moment. Sometimes, she lives alone and sometimes with her man.

Her beauty is overwhelming in her man's eyes. She may let that go to her head, figuring that she can have anybody she wants. But, in this case, she lives with her man.

The guy is down to earth, usually laughing and joking. But, when it is time to get serious, he is on point.

Like her man, she wears two faces.

Her man works hard and tries to do everything in his power to keep her happy. She agrees with most everything he says. She keeps her house in order.

She loves to be in the spotlight and he likes hanging around his boys—in clubs or wherever. He does not do anything to jeopardize his relationship with his woman.

She puts on her other face. She changes like a chameleon: Where are you going? You don't need to be around your boys anymore. Why do you have to go to the club? Why this? Why that?

She begins hanging around as though they were one person. She does not want the telephone to ring. If it does, she races him to answer it first. If he gets it first, she is all in his mouth on every word.

She gets upset when his friend comes around. She begins to get upset with everything he does. She wants to control him in every way that she can.

If they go out, she wants him to hold his head down just to keep him from looking at somebody else. He has no say-so any more. She cuts him off when he tries to talk.

When he gets tired of her wickedness, he decides to terminate the relationship. He moves out and gets an apartment to have peace of mind. He thinks he is free. No such luck.

She finds out where he lives. She stalks him frequently. She knocks on his door. She tries to break into his apartment. She "goes off" like a mad woman. She follows him everywhere he goes. He does not know it.

She cannot take no for an answer. Morning, noon, and night, she comes on his job trying to win his love back. She cannot take it anymore. She cannot believe that it is over.

She is about to go out of her mind. She does not listen to anybody. Her mind becomes blocked and she cannot see anybody but him. If he talks to another woman, she pops up from nowhere and tries to fight the woman.

She cannot see herself moving on. She will inflict pain on herself just to draw attention. She tries anything she can think of to get attention. Sometimes, she gets into her car and just drives without having a destination in mind.

She is thinking about hurting herself.

He finds his automobile windows broken out, the doors to his apartment smashed in. She wants revenge. Nothing else matters.

Will she ever come to her senses and end the drama? Do you think she needs help or will it eventually go away on its own?

The Possessive Man

This man comes with all the answers you want to hear. But he is two-faced.

You see face Number 1 when he first meets you. He pretends to be laid back. He will try everything in the book to draw you into his web.

The woman sees the first face and begins to let herself go. She starts clinging to him.

He takes her to the movies, dinner and whatever draws her further into his web He sits back and observes every move she makes and every step she takes.

He is a pretender, covers her like a coat. The woman does not take time to observe his moods. All she sees is the face. She becomes more and more attached.

Now Face No. 2 appears. Now she is in his web. Suddenly, he does not want her to go out. She has no freedom because he is always around, always under foot. She can only wear clothes he wants her to wear.

She cannot talk on the phone when he is present. She cannot talk on the phone when he is not there. She cannot talk to her family. She cannot do anything on her own any more. His mind has become her mind or is it the other way around.

The result is the same. She is strangling in his shrinking web. She is beautiful. She has a beautiful face and body, but he tells her: I can mess up that face and that body so nobody else will want you.

Now he is complaining that she is in the spotlight a lot because of the business she owns and operates. He cannot take it any more and wants her to close the business.

When she refuses, he becomes abusive. He becomes Dr. Jekyll and Mr. Hyde. She really does not know what to do. She wants to get out of this relationship but she is afraid. She is always looking over her shoulder because of his threats: If you leave me, I am going to kill you. If I cannot have you, nobody else can.

He has driven her to the edge. She is in the last stages of having a nervous breakdown. She becomes more nervous and afraid. What do you do in this situation?

When she finally "breaks" and hurts him, the law cannot see it. She has been reporting his threats to the police for months but she has been ignored. When does the law really work for the abused? When does the law work for anybody?

Why are these men like this? Are they possessed? Do they really see themselves as possessive?

The Intimidated Man

When a man meets a woman that is secure, why does he become intimidated? This woman has her own business and just about every material thing she wants. But, a man that she wants to love and spend her life with, she has not found.

She knows all too well that material things do not take the place of being in love and sharing your love with someone else. She is not looking for someone to "control." That is not on her mind.

The man's mind takes a bad turn. Because he feels she is successful, insecurity sets in. She does not know it. He feels that he has no say so in matters because she makes more money than he does. Is this stupidity or weakness or both?

When they first met, he did not feel that way. Everything was good and the relationship was going good. All he could see was her face and her beauty. He just saw her, not the material things.

Later, when he finds out that her payroll is more than his, he becomes furious. He becomes insecure instead of being grateful and seeing her as his blessing and as someone that has shown and proven her love to him.

She does not look at him thinking that he is less than a man. She is looking at him with admiration. She wants to share herself and everything that she possesses with him—her one and only man. Instead of fulfilling that role, he becomes a jerk.

Such men make weaklings of themselves when they fail to do their part and let everything fall into place. They are always thinking negative things about a woman but cannot see that the shortcoming is in themselves.

She has opened the door for you to be the man that she is seeking; she wants you to take charge. So, who is running who, where? Men let your woman be her own woman. Women let your man be a man. You should be each other's backbone.

Because she is secure, life doesn't stop there. Although she has set her goals early and made it, life has just begun for her. The right man, you, is the missing piece. Her success makes it hard for her to find someone who is just going to see her as her.

Neither most women nor most men want to be controlling. If a man feels insecure when he meets a woman, he should not get into a relationship with her.

Some men want to be in control at all cost. They are "old school" thinkers: Men are suppose to provide for the family and the woman is only there to take care of the children and the household.

Everything worked out "back then" because most men had a purpose in life. They provided the best they could and when things got rough she had his back.

What happened?

Things changed in a big way in the world of relationships. Focus on what is good for the family has shifted to where both parties today want to be in control. For both, everything is about me and mine.

Many men change the moment a woman becomes self-secure. They wonder: What does she need me for? If he had any dreams of his own, they vanish at that moment.

He becomes helpless in his own mind thinking that he has no purpose and has become a failure with things he has never tried. He forgets that she accepted him for what she saw in him not for what she thought he had.

When his insecurity gets the best of him, he cannot take it anymore. Jealousy takes over and no one can tell him the situation is not as he is picturing it. Pretty soon, he starts "tripping" and everything gets distorted in his mind.

Instead of going on and trying to prove that he is the man she is looking for, he turns negative and thinks: What can I tell this person who has everything? His mind is so shallow, he does not realize that he can just bring himself to the table.

Women seem to be less likely to be intimidated when the situation is reversed. They tend to give their all to help her man reach his goals. Too often, what they get in return after he has reached his dream is hurt and lack of appreciation.

She is put on the back burner or told outright: I don't need you now. Now she is too stressed out to remember what goals she had set for herself, once-upon-a-time. Now she is thinking for the most part: This man has made a fool out of me. I want revenge.

How can you mistreat someone that you love so dearly? Was it really love in the beginning or did he find someone to get over on for his own gain? She put all her trust in her man believing each would help the other reach their goals but he looks out only for himself.

Insecure men need to come to their senses before it is too late and realize that no one owes them anything. The real question is: What do you owe yourself?

Everything happens for a reason . . .

Wendell Walker

Is It Me Or Is It You?

Chapter Four

Show Me Some Love . . .

—4—
CHAPTER

Show Me Some Love . . .

How a Woman Is Suppose to Be Treated

When life opens your eyes to see a world of beauty and amazement, joy comes into your heart. As teenagers when boy meets girl and girl meets boy, puppy love makes the heart pump, even skip a beat.

First they want each other's phone number or address. They cannot wait for the first call. They cannot eat or sleep, waiting on that call. The wait seems like weeks and months although it has only been two days.

During the first conversation, they do not know what to say. But soon a few words come out and, after a few days, they are laughing and talking with confidence. Then the magic words are spoken: I like you. I like you too. Can I be your boyfriend? Yes.

It is as if heaven has opened its doors. School love seems to be serious until school years end. Some lead to marriage, others become lifetime memories, and some just fade away forever.

What makes some people connect at first sight? What makes some people be so "distant" and difficult to approach? What makes us connect? What makes us fall in love? How can love sometimes turn to hate?

What makes us change when we find out that a certain someone is not the one for us, when we are convinced that the grass is greener on the other side of the fence? What leads a person to dump the one they are with and head for the greener pasture?

Very often, after a couple of months go by, girlfriend or boyfriend regrets the decision. Now, they are as miserable as the person they dumped. They try to turn back the hands of time but it is too late. The old flame is taken.

Such experiences in the teen or early adult years sometime leave emotional scars and give birth to bad attitudes that stay with both parties for years if not a lifetime.

What happens when they grow into adults? No one ever quite measures up to expectations because that "first love" keeps clouding the picture. Phony expectations can kill all hope of building a healthy relationship.

Meeting and getting off to a good start does not need to be that hard. God did the hard part during creation. Women are creatures of beauty. God's work with a woman was perfect. He did not do all that badly with the man.

Men and women need to look for the beauty—as God created it—in each other when they meet and then go from there. Of course, that does not refer to skin-deep physical "beauty" that a person can let go to their head.

When you meet, just be yourself from the beginning and no surprises will come up to cause trouble later.

Find out about likes and dislikes, life purposes and goals; be open—minded and listen to each other.

Talk about what makes you laugh. You may be surprised at where this conversation alone will take you.

How Are You Treated By A Man

Why does a man want a woman that he wants to control? He cannot cook so she has to do all of that for him. He never wants her to go anywhere because he is jealous. If he calls and the phone rings more than five times, he gets upset. He wants to control your whole life.

She has a college degree, a purpose in life and clear goals. But the man wants her to do nothing but be within arms-reach when he wants her. She has no say, it is all about him. She gets no respect as a woman, especially as "his" woman.

Why not become a real man? What did you do to get her in the beginning? Remember how you went out of your way to please? You found time that the clock did not have. You squeezed an hour out of every ten minutes.

What made you change? If you had continued to treat her like a queen, you would not be so jealous. Treat her now the way you would want to be treated if you were in her shoes. For example:

Let her be her own woman. She has a mind of her own. Let her have her freedom. Stop looking around the corner trying to see where see went. She knows her way home.

Show your love for her openly and often. Remember that you need each other. Do not down her because your mind is ahead of hers in some things. Keep your feelings for her real. Do not look at yourself as the boss, even if you pay the bills.

Be a good companion. Try to keep her smiling and laughing. Women like to be cuddled. They want to hear you say "I love you" other than when you are having sex. Let saying it be your routine.

Let her know that you appreciate everything she does for you. Thank her for just being there for you. Thank her for putting up with you. Make her feel wanted and a vital part of your life.

When you come home from work and she meets you at the door looking like a queen and smelling good just for you, do not let the first thing out of your mouth be "Where are you going? instead of "You look beautiful" or "All of this just for me?

When you make a mistake and ask her for forgiveness, she gives it. Follow suit when it is the other way around. She is not suddenly a "bitch or whore" or any other nasty name you can think of. Say what you have to say and leave it. Leave it where you started it.

How A Controlling Woman Treats You

Are you controlling? Do you want to be the boss?

When you are independent, do you feel that you should control everything?

A man wants to be treated as your King. He works hard, sometimes long hours, so that you all can live a modern life. He brings his paycheck home, gives it to you—and still gets mistreated.

He is mostly a "yes man" and agrees with you just for the sake of avoiding an argument. You take your "control" for granted. You tell him what to eat and wear and when to do this and that.

A lot of such women are still alone. Wonder why? There is a better way. For example:

Make him feel like a man. If you have any love for him—not just for yourself—show it. Think: God created this man just for me and I am going to worship the ground he walks on. I will praise him to the highest and, when he is down, I will be there for him.

Look at your relationship this way: God just gave me all the keys to heaven—not just for me or just for him, but for the both of you.

Man's Duties To Keep His Woman

1. Let your woman know that you love her.

2. Women like to be told frequently that you love her.

3. Women like to be held.

4. Women like to be kissed.

5. Women like to feel secure at all times.

6. Women like sex, only when she says so.

7. Treat her like a queen.

8. Give her shopping money, if you can afford it.

9. Take care of home.

10. Meet your responsibility, at home and abroad.

11. Women want your respect as a man.

12. They want their freedom.

13. Make them feel that they are the only one on earth that can keep you going.

Woman's Duties To Keep Her Man

1. Treat your man like a king.

2. Respect him at all times.

3. Make him feel needed.

4. Make him feel secure.

5. Make him feel your love for him.

6. Give him space; some need a little, some need a lot.

7. Let him be his own boss.

8. Sometimes, men do not need as much as women.

9. Make him feel responsible for you.

Shopping

Who does the most shopping in your household? Sometimes it is the man but usually it is the woman. She likes shopping more than she likes Jesus.

She buys when she has the money and shops when she does not have the money. Her whole life revolves around shopping and she charges to the max. She owns stuff she does not even get to wear.

Shopping is as much an addiction as drugs but she (or he) does not realize it. The situation calls to mind the old saying: I didn't have any clothes when I was coming up and I promised myself that when I get grown I am going to buy whatever I want.

If you are frustrated, you shop. If you are lonely, worried, or lose your appetite, you shop some more.

You have run out of storage space, so now you want the one closet your man has been using.

You do not have space for anything else in the house because every room already looks like Macy's furniture department. That may work for now but how about later when it is time to retire?

Your retirement check will be so small you will have trouble seeing it. If you had put one third of your shopping money away, you could have retired at an early age and been secure.

You have spent all your money and his. Now you are getting ready to lose your house and car because you live in your clothes.

Banking On Whose Money?

Why do couples have a problem with who makes the most money? If the woman makes more than the man does, he has a problem. What makes him feel that he is less than a man or feel that he has no say so?

He feels th

Chapter Five

DON'T GO CHANGING, NOT FOR NOTHING . . .

—5—
CHAPTER

Don't Go Changing, Not for Nothing . . .

Changes

What is love? Why do we use that word so freely? What causes a man and a woman to click from the beginning? What runs through their minds when they first lay eyes upon each other?

Sometimes, what they really want at the moment is just sex but they "play it off". They come up with the big lie: I just want to get to know you. When rejection comes, the mind shifts gears and the bad vibes fly in all directions.

If people could just speak their true minds when they meet, maybe true love would not be so hard to find. Most of the time, we try to impress each other with material things. When the real truth comes out, "love" turns out to be a Catch 22 situation.

We should go into a relationship with an open mind and heart. Then, win, lose, or draw, at least you were honest with yourself. That way, you don't have to worry so much and work so hard to keep your lies straight.

Sometimes, a person in a relationship changes suddenly and for no apparent reason. Why? Was it something I said, did, or did not do? Or were you living out a lie from the beginning?

People in general lie a lot. A person who is not accustomed to dealing with liars gets hurt the worst. Others are so attuned to hearing lies, they don't know how to take it when someone is being truthful. Their negative mind cannot handle it.

Sometimes people are afraid to be themselves. They think they have to live a make-believe life to make it.

They live out a life-long joke. When they realize real life has passed them by, it is too late to change. It is time to retire.

Set goals in life and follow your plan. Stay focused and let no one deter you from your dreams. The same rules apply to relationships. Of course, you can't "plan" everything but go as far as you can and then let nature take its course.

Why We Do the Things We Do

A man and a woman meet; they look at each other and their minds seem to interlock. They share a desire to do so much for each other. They come with promises that they cannot keep.

They do things instinctively and expect nothing in return. They act on impulse like a person who sees someone drowning and jumps into the water without thinking. They are thinking about saving a soul, not about themselves.

Instinct has its place and purpose in life and in a developing relationship.

Now, the man and woman have established a solid connection. They want to do things that are out of the ordinary. They want to do things that reflect love and caring. Each is anxious to respond to the other's every beck and call.

Sometimes, one or both will do something looking to get something out of it. They become takers. Sometimes, that develops into a habit.

Jealousy

Has anyone ever found the real meaning of jealousy? What is that emotion or trait that can cause a person to change so drastically, sometimes in an instant, and behave so badly?

Take the woman, for instance. You meet her and, in your eyes, she is divine. You pour your all and all into her and she accepts it all. She is truthful to you in all her ways and you feel the same toward her.

Then, she begins to do things that make you uncomfortable. The way she talks to you takes on a tone that says: Deep down in my heart, I feel that

I can do anything I want to and you should not say anything.

Take the man. At first, he is down to earth and loving. He is not argumentative and shows no signs of being abusive.

Then he becomes both and more. Is it because he is being treated like dirt or is it something else—jealousy or envy, maybe?

Possessions and accomplishments are two things that can bring out jealousy and envy in a relationship. One person resents the other for what they have or have achieved. They do not understand or appreciate what the person has put into getting where they are.

Sometimes, the jealous person does not seem to reason things out at all. They simply want to be the other person and act as if they believe they deserve to have what the other person has. They seem convinced that they are not getting their fair share of the other person's success.

Jealousy is powerful. It makes a person do things they would not ordinarily do: stalking, peeping around corners to see where a companion is going, looking into their personal things, checking their e-mails, phone calls and mail box.

A person operating in a jealous state is weak. They are easily influenced by the chatter of relatives, friends, and the general public whose comments are sometimes well-meaning but most often just mean-spirited or down-right evil. If a person is really weak, the stress can lead them to commit a crime.

When a man and a woman meet, everything appears to be in order. If we could only see the future and stop it before it starts.

Obsession

Here is a couple that has been in a relationship for a few years. They were so in love with each other that they thought their lives would end together. Now the woman has thrown him a curve. The relationship is starting to get out of hand.

The man begins to go out of his way to keep her. He begs her to stay but she does not want to hear anything he has to say.

He gives her money that he does not have, follows her around, goes to her work place, and stalks her. She is not swayed and makes it clear she still does not want to hear what he has to say.

Jealousy and desperation set in. He cannot eat, sleep or work. He feels his whole life is slipping away. He does not know what to do. He considers murder and suicide: If I kill her and myself, I do not have to worry about anyone else having her.

Some women react the same way in such a situation. She breaks the windows in his car, cuts up his clothes, begins to argue a lot; wants to fight every woman he looks at. She does not want him to go anywhere.

She shows up where he is unexpectedly and she too proclaims: No other woman is going to have you.

These people have been "shacking" for ten years or more but do not want to get married. Marriage sounds like something nasty to them. Finding someone else would seem to be the next logical step but obsession has taken control of the situation.

The next person entering a relationship with either of the persons involved is going to catch hell.

What Makes Men Go Astray?

Why does the man feel ashamed when he has loss his job? On the job he has bragged that he is the captain of his ship. What makes him afraid to tell his mate? Why did he not save for a rainy day when he was working?

Now this ambitious man has become a home sitter and feels that he cannot do anything else. Instead of looking for another job, he just lets his life go down the drain.

His mate gets frustrated with him. She is ready to leave. Should she stick with him for a while longer or is she doing the right thing?

Why did his pride go down the drain? Sometimes, the situation leads to drinking, getting hooked on drugs and other activities that take a man down.

When the good woman tries to pick him up, she is rejected. He loses all control and seems to think that she is the cause of his set back.

What Makes Women Wander?

Her man gives her his heart, soul and mind. He takes care of home, bills and her. She is his royal queen and does not want for anything.

She goes on the other side of the fence.

She is never satisfied.

He never gets sex from her but everybody else does.

She begins to drain their bank account and gives it to the other man or she turns lesbian.

Most of the time they become satisfied when the other man or woman treats her like hell.

A woman that had everything, she ends up going to the dogs.

What happened?

If we could only see the future and stop it before it starts.

Wendell Walker

Is It Me Or Is It You?

Chapter Six

CONCLUSION

—6—
CHAPTER

CONCLUSION

What Now?

After you have read this book and met a variety of men women handling or mishandling a wide range of situations, what are you going to do to make your relationship better?

Are you going to think about your faults and try to improve them or accept what you are doing as okay?

There are many positive things in this book. If they applytoyoursituation—pleasantlyorotherwise—you would do well to "... think on these things ..."

If you have already made up your minds to continue doing what you are doing, consider this: Your man or woman has feelings just as you do. Would you want yours hurt? Think.

A man and a woman should stick together and lift each other up in a relationship. If one or the other starts, maybe the other one will join in. None of us is perfect, just striving to get there. We know this or should.

Every person has been put on this earth for a reason. If a person is clear about what their purpose is in life and has set some goals, finding someone with whom to build a relationship comes more easily.

It cost you nothing to map out a plan for achieving your dreams. A plan makes it more difficult for anyone or anything to deter you along the way.

Here is the trick to the thing: Put that first foot forward and slide the other one up. That is one step. You have made a start whether it is life you are taking on or that next glorious relationship.

You do not know who will be put into your path to help you. Advice will come out of the blue, knowledge that will advance you will begin to pop up.

Now—ready or not—your mate should embrace and encourage you and be thankful to you for making a move.

Pick out the qualities that you like in this book and use them to keep a spark going in your relationship. The bad scenes have been presented to make you think: How can I avoid repeating my mistakes. Sometimes we do not realize what we are doing.

If you stumbled across yourself in this book, communicate with the man or woman in your life. Say this: I did not know that I was causing you all this pain. Let's just take one day at a time and make up for the mistakes. Let's let the past stay in the past and start at the now.

We know that life is a mystery. Sometimes, we have to act on instinct and try to enjoy every breath and every heartbeat. With that done, we will discover that just living is a lot of fun and sharing doubles the pleasure. A lot of love will surface on its own when we follow our heart.

Here is the trick to the thing: Put that first foot forward and slide the other one up. That is one step.

Wendell Walker

Is It Me Or Is It You?

MORE ABOUT THE AUTHOR

HIS FIRST BOOK

Is It Me Or Is It You is the second book authored by Wendell Walker in a three-year period. His first, published by AuthorHouse (Bloomington, IN, 2007) was entitled The Real Deal About Real Estate (No Crap).

As its title promises, the volume presents an authoritative "insider's" view of what it takes to make it in real estate—especially if your largest asset at the outset is a dream.

In Real Deal, Walker's inspiring account of his ". . . rise to success . . ." moves simultaneously along two paths—success in life and success in business.

The book's Forward notes:

In life he moves up from being one of 17 siblings in a poor, Roanoke, VA family and being educated at times in a four-room school heated by potbelly stoves.

In business, the rise is similar. As a Vietnam War veteran, he builds a mini-financial empire on $2 cash, his fare from Tacoma, WA to Baltimore, and faith—in God and himself.

In addition to the inspiring story line, Real Deal offers pages of practical, simply-stated business tips, hints and guidelines.

To order a copy of The Real Deal About Real Estate (No Crap), contact: AuthorHouse, Book Department, at 1-888-280-7715 or visit www.AuthorHouse.com

FAMILY MAN, MAN OF FAITH

Walker's devotion to family is deep and abiding. He has endured difficult circumstances but came through with his belief in the importance of family intact. He is equally firm in his view of God's place in life in general and in man's pursuit of success and happiness.

His first marriage ended on a sad note in 1978. One year after having moved into their first home and the birth of their first child, a girl, his wife died. He had the challenge of rearing the baby and two step children.

"We learned to take care of each other," he says now to emphasize what he sees as a key block in building a sound family.

He remarried two years later. "My new wife understood my existing family needs and she grasped my vision," he says today. His point is clear: Family means understanding and supporting each other no matter what.

Whether celebrating his success or recounting the rough road he travelled to get there, Walker frequently acknowledges his debt to God. "I had to reach deep inside for the faith and strength to keep going," he says when recalling the day an effort to help a friend buy a house was on the brink of collapse.

The deal worked out. Walker is not bashful in giving God the credit, for that and all of the ". . . bountiful . . . blessings . . ." that have come ". . . along the way."

"Thank God for everything because He is your guide and He is always at hand," Walker declares. "You never know who will be placed in your path (by Him) to accelerate the journey or just to point you down the right path."

SELF-MADE ENTREPRENEUR

"Harvest Time" is how Wendell Walker cheerfully labels the pinnacle of success he now enjoys as a business man. Years ago, he exceeded his original dream, which was to acquire 20 properties. His current holdings include ownership and operation of a Health Spa and Dance School.

The journey has taken more than 40 years. It continues to unfold daily as his now—familiar van crisscrosses Baltimore boldly declaring:

WALKER'S
HOME IMPROVEMENT CO.
"THE MAN WITH THE HAMMER"

The trek began in 1967 with an attempt to form a two-man, house painting partnership. The partner-to-be backed out. A later try at creating a six-man venture capital group also went awry. Going it alone and working out of his basement at home, Walker acquired his home improvement license in 1968.

To build on his thriving home improvement business, Walker began to buy real estate in 1970. His first purchase was a house and lot for which he paid $2,500. He expanded the effort in 1972 and continued to do so from 1983 to 2003.

In 2007, Walker discovered a new investment opportunity with the U.S. Department of Housing and Urban Development (HUD). His first venture in this area was a $25,000 house which he managed to finance without going to a bank.

A highpoint in the journey came in 1999 with the purchase of an $89,000 condo in Myrtle Beach, SC and, a few days later, acquisition of the $140,000 building that he later retro-fitted to house his Health Spa and Dance School.

MULTI-TALENTED, MULTI-TASKER

The author's defining trademark is not his business savvy and success. It is his wide range of abilities and interests. He is multi-dimensional, a Renaissance Man, a People Person.

A largely self-taught musician, he plays the organ or piano Sundays at his church and on other special occasions as needed. He serves free of charge. In high school, he was a drummer in the band.

He learned to play the piano and organ as a young man hanging out in Baltimore night clubs. He watched and mingled with the performers. He learned enough to play with a few bands and later formed a band of his own. He also sang with a local gospel quartet for a time and is currently a member of the Male Chorus at his church.

He teaches kung fu. He uses his knowledge and skill in the field to give back to the community. His main focus is to teach young people the importance of self-discipline and physical and mental fitness.

An avid reader, he loves to explore "old" versions of the Bible and the writings of little-known philosophers whose works he has somehow acquired. He "quotes" from both freely in friendly conversations—mostly for laughs or their "shock" effect.

His own philosophy of life—which he shares freely and forcefully with anyone willing to listen—revolves around a few core values—vision and goal setting, self-reliance, truthfulness and honesty, sharing, and helping others.

He has helped many people. "You don't have to wait until you 'reach the top' before you help somebody . . . Sharing myself with other dreamers has been wonderful."

at he should be the man of the house and should be taking care of his family. Life does not come with directions. He should stop looking at what she makes and what he makes. Think instead that we are a team.

Life is not one-sided unless you choose it. If you feel that you cannot cope with her making more than you, leave and stop the drama. Some men cannot deal with reality. They fear they cannot control her if her income is bigger than his.

She probably is not the problem, he is. She feels that she is taking a big load off of him. She brings more to the table because this is what she wants, not for herself, but for the both of you.

The man gropes around, looking like a zombie and feeling guilty or knocks himself out until he finds a job that pays more. The job may come with conditions—location, working hours, for example—that cause her to leave him.

Money did not bring you all together in the first place. In the beginning, neither knew or cared a great deal about who made what. Why act the fool about it later? Remember, a fool and his money will soon part.

Is it because of "peer pressure." Are you afraid that your buddies or so-called friends will make fun of you? Are you getting frustrated because their jokes keep coming: "Hey man, she doesn't need you. What your poor ass hanging around for?"

Now you are thinking all kinds of things, like hurting her or doing something else you will live to regret. How did it come to this? You probably have yourself to thank.

The size of your incomes is between the two of you. How would your "buddies" know anything about it? The lesson is simple. Sometimes you just need to keep your mouth shut.

Life is not one-sided unless you choose it.

Wendell Walker

Is It Me Or Is It You?

Wendell Walker

www.ingramcontent.com/pod-product-compliance
Lightning Source LLC
Chambersburg PA
CBHW051448280526
45785CB00003B/1478